TRINITY GRAMMAR JUNIOR SCHOOL

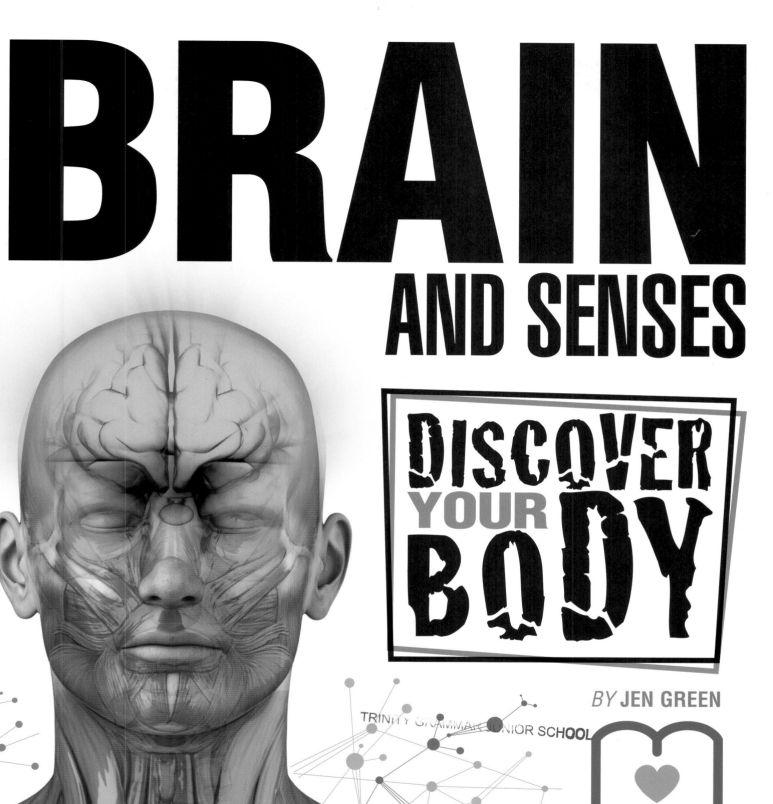

BRAIN
AND SENSES

DISCOVER
YOUR BODY

BY JEN GREEN

BookLife

THIS EDITION:
© 2015
BOOK LIFE
KING'S LYNN
NORFOLK PE30 4LS

FIRST EDITION:
GREAT BRITAIN IN 2003
© ALADDIN BOOKS LTD.
PO BOX 53987
LONDON SW15 2SF

ISBN:
978-1-910512-05-0

DESIGNED BY:
IAN McMULLEN
& MATT RUMBELOW

ILLUSTRATORS:
AZIZ A. KHAN,
SIMON MORSE,
ROB SHONE,
IAN THOMPSON
CERTAIN ILLUSTRATIONS
HAVE APPEARED IN
EARLIER BOOKS CREATED
BY ALADDIN BOOKS.

MEDICAL EDITOR:
DR HILARY PINNOCK
DR PINNOCK IS A GP WORKING
IN WHITSTABLE, KENT. SHE HAS
WRITTEN AND CONSULTED ON
A WIDE VARIETY OF MEDICAL
PUBLICATIONS FOR ALL AGES.

CONTENTS

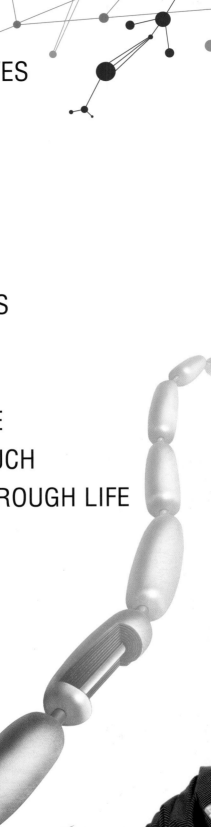

INTRODUCTION

You are the proud owner of one of the most sophisticated machines in the known universe – the human brain. Your brain is at work right now, not only allowing you to read this book but also keeping your body ticking over. Your senses are also amazing, providing you with all kinds of information about the world around you. Read on to find out more about your incredible brain and senses, and how to take good care of them.

MEDICAL TOPIC

Follow the red heart icon to find out about different medical conditions and the effects that they can have on the human body.

YOU AND YOUR BRAIN

The brain icon indicates areas where you can find out how you can help improve your general health and keep your brain and senses in tiptop condition.

HEALTH FACTS & HEALTH TIPS

Look for the apple icon to find out more about the different parts of your body and how they work. These boxes also give you tips on how to keep yourself really healthy.

YOUR BRAIN AND NERVES

A BRAIN IS A MASS OF NERVE CELLS LINKED TO OTHER NERVES THROUGHOUT THE BODY. A JELLYFISH HAS A NERVE NETWORK BUT NO BRAIN AS SUCH.

Your brain is one of the most vital organs in your body. It acts as a control centre that directs all the other parts, allowing you to move, solve problems, remember and feel. The brain is linked to the rest of the body through a network of nerves. The brain and all the nerves together form the nervous system. Animals such as dolphins (right) also have a well-developed nervous system.

SYSTEMS OF THE BODY

Body systems are the body's main working units. They help each other to work. The circulatory system supplies the brain with oxygen from the respiratory (breathing) system and nourishment from the digestive system.

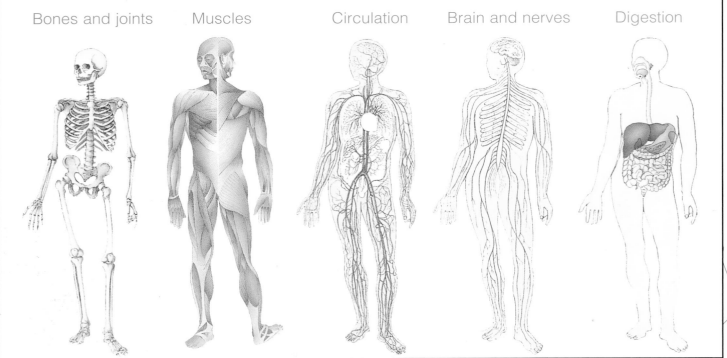

Bones and joints   Muscles   Circulation   Brain and nerves   Digestion

THE NERVOUS SYSTEM

The spinal cord runs down inside your backbone. It is a bundle of nerves that connects your brain to different parts of the body. The brain and spinal cord form the central nervous system. The network of smaller nerves throughout the body is called the peripheral nervous system.

BRAIN

SPINAL CORD

NERVES

COORDINATING SENSES AND MOVEMENT

Information from your senses, such as the sight of a moving ball, travels along nerves to your brain. In response, the brain may send signals via nerves to your muscles, so that you can catch the ball.

NERVES ENDING AT THE SKIN

CONSCIOUS AND UNCONSCIOUS

Your brain takes care of unconscious processes like breathing and digestion without you even being aware of it. It also allows you to carry out all sorts of conscious processes such as: working out problems, making decisions and having a good time!

WHAT A NERVE!

A network of nerves reaches every part of your body. The sciatic nerve is the thickest and longest nerve in the body. It is about 2cm across when it leaves the spinal cord and its longest fibres reach all the way down to your toes.

YOUR SENSES

Your senses allow you to experience what is going on around you. They relay information about sights, smells, sounds, tastes and touch sensations to the brain, which sorts and processes the data. In addition to the five main senses, you also have other sensors throughout your body. Some of these sensors help you balance, others warn that the body is low in oxygen or needs food and water.

THE FIVE SENSES

Four of the five main senses, sight, hearing, smell and taste, are based in specialised sense organs in your head – your eyes, ears, nose and mouth. The fifth sense, touch, depends on sensors located throughout the skin that forms your body's outer surface. Some parts of your skin are much more sensitive than others.

HEARING

Hearing enables you to detect sounds including speech, allowing you to communicate with others. It makes you aware of loud noises that may spell danger, and also lets you enjoy music.

TOUCH

Touch is a complicated sense made up of many different sensations. Sensors in your skin detect heat, cold, pressure, vibrations, itchiness, soreness and pain. Your sense of touch also allows you to distinguish between different textures.

 ## SKIN CARE

As well as the sense of touch, your skin provides a vital barrier between you and the outside world. Skin is easily damaged by exposure to sunlight. Remember to put on plenty of sunscreen to keep your skin healthy whenever you are in the sun.

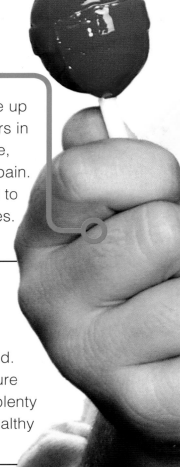

SIGHT

Two-thirds of all the information in your brain arrives via your eyes. As well as giving vital information about your surroundings and other people, vision also allows you to absorb information in the form of words, pictures and diagrams.

SMELL

Your sense of smell allows you to appreciate pleasant scents such as flowers – and also detect not-so-pleasant pongs, such as the whiff of gas or bad food. In this way, your sense of smell helps to keep you safe and healthy.

TASTE

What's your favourite food? Your sense of taste allows you to enjoy it. Working with the sense of smell, taste can also tell you when food is 'off' and best avoided.

THE BRAIN

Your brain fills the upper part of your head. This soft, spongy organ, mostly made of water, is protected by the bony case of your skull. Your brain is made up of billions of nerve cells all connected to one another. The outer layer of the brain, called the cerebral cortex, is wrinkled like the shell of a walnut, so that even more brain cells can be packed in!

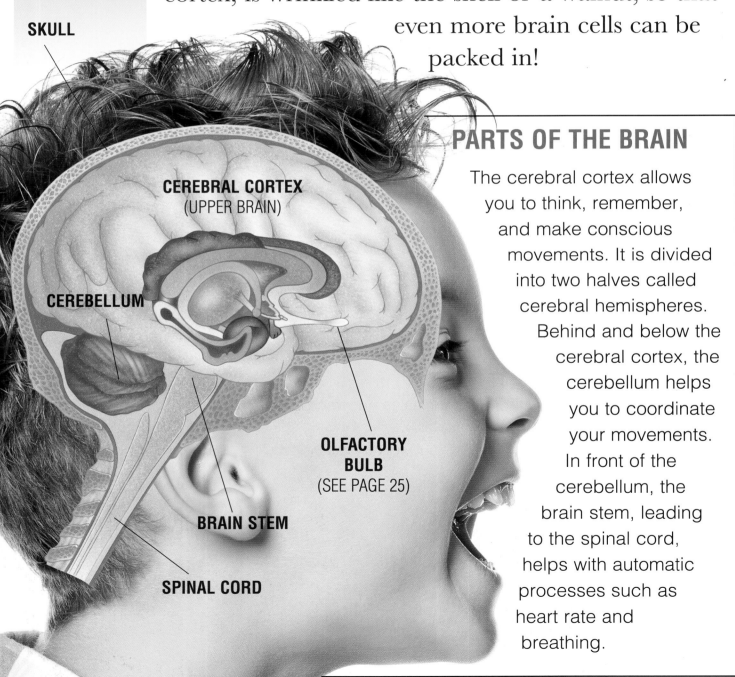

SKULL

CEREBRAL CORTEX
(UPPER BRAIN)

CEREBELLUM

OLFACTORY
BULB
(SEE PAGE 25)

BRAIN STEM

SPINAL CORD

PARTS OF THE BRAIN

The cerebral cortex allows you to think, remember, and make conscious movements. It is divided into two halves called cerebral hemispheres. Behind and below the cerebral cortex, the cerebellum helps you to coordinate your movements. In front of the cerebellum, the brain stem, leading to the spinal cord, helps with automatic processes such as heart rate and breathing.

THE NERVOUS SYSTEM

The brain only makes up about one-fiftieth of your body weight, yet it uses one-fifth of your blood supply. Blood, pumped from the heart to the brain along arteries (shown in red), supplies brain cells with vital oxygen, glucose for energy and also nutrients (nourishment). The brain uses up energy whether you are awake or asleep. Other blood vessels, called veins (shown in blue) carry blood and waste products away.

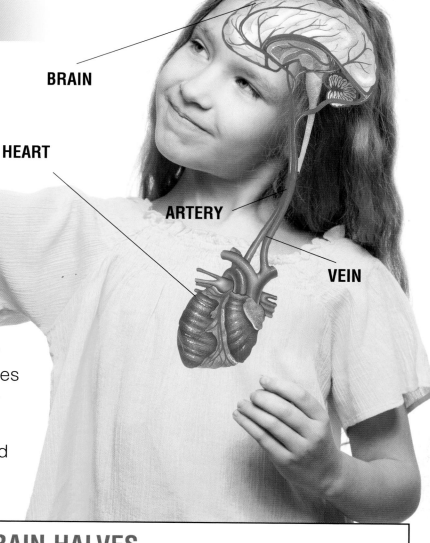

BRAIN

HEART

ARTERY

VEIN

INTO THE UNKNOWN

Scientists are starting to understand more about the brain but we still know relatively little about how it really works. For example, no-one really knows how memories form, or what happens to your brain while you're asleep.

BRAIN HALVES

The two halves of the upper brain can be seen in this angiogram, which shows the brain's arteries. Here you can see that the right side of the brain has been injured. In a healthy brain, the left side of the brain usually dominates during problem-solving, writing and number work. The right side usually takes the lead during creative activities.

BRAIN PROTECTION

The brain is a vital, but also delicate organ. The tough case of your skull, and also the skin of your head help protect your brain from minor bumps and injuries. Activities such as cycling and skateboarding may deliver more serious knocks. Wear a helmet to protect your brain when doing any dangerous sport. Better to be safe than sorry!

CAFFEINE

Caffeine, found in cola, tea and coffee, is a drug that affects brain activity. Caffeine speeds up brain activity, making you more alert for a while. Taken in moderation, caffeine has not been shown to harm your health.

THE BRAIN AT WORK

The cerebral cortex is the 'thinking brain'. Conscious thought and feelings take place in this wrinkly, outer layer of the cerebrum. The grey matter of the cerebral cortex, made up of millions of nerve cell bodies, covers the white matter of nerve connections that form the bulk of the cerebrum. Memories are formed in the cerebral cortex and also in an area called the hippocampus, which lies deep within the brain.

MEMORY GAMES

Test a friend's memory by assembling a collection of objects like those shown below. Let your friend study the objects for half a minute, and then cover them up with a cloth. How many objects can he or she remember?

BRAIN WAVES

Electrical activity in the brain shows up as wavy lines or 'brain waves' on a machine called an electro-encephalograph (EEG). The wave patterns vary according to whether the brain is more or less active.
Rapid Eye Movement (REM) sleep occurs when you dream and your brain is quite active. During deep sleep your brain waves are deeper and slower.

AWAKE

REM SLEEP

DEEP SLEEP

SPEECH CENTRE

The speech centre allows you to produce speech. The Wernicke's area allows you to understand what other people are saying.

HEARING CENTRES

Part of the cerebral cortex, called the auditory centre, receives signals from the ears and makes sense of them, so you can hear sounds.

TOUCH CENTRES

This sensory centre receives messages from sensors in your skin to register heat, pain, pressure and other sensations.

MOVEMENT CENTRES

The motor cortex is a zone running over the top of the brain. It is here that your brain plans movements and transmits signals to muscles, which move your limbs.

SIGHT CENTRES

Signals from your eyes are processed in the visual centre at the rear of the cerebral cortex so that you can make sense of what you see.

PARKINSON'S DISEASE

Parkinson's disease is an illness that affects certain cells in the brain stem. People with this illness tremble and have difficulty controlling their movements. For some brain diseases it can be useful to use a PET scanner to monitor brain activity, with the help of a radioactive dye.

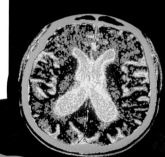

ZONES OF THE OUTER BRAIN

Particular areas of the cerebral cortex are linked with sensation and movement. The various sensory centres process signals from sense organs such as eyes and ears. More than one area of the brain can be involved in one function. For example, the brain has two hearing centres. One detects sound quality – pitch and loudness – and the other makes sense of the information.

MOVEMENT

TOUCH

EMOTION AND COMPLEX THOUGHT

SPEECH

SIGHT

HEARING

CEREBELLUM

WERNICKE'S AREA

BRAIN STEM

SPINAL CORD

YOUR SPINAL CORD

The spinal cord, your body's main bundle of nerves, is about as thick as your finger. Signals from touch sensors in the skin, and instructions from the brain all pass along the spinal cord. It is involved in lightning-fast responses called reflex actions, which help protect you from harm.

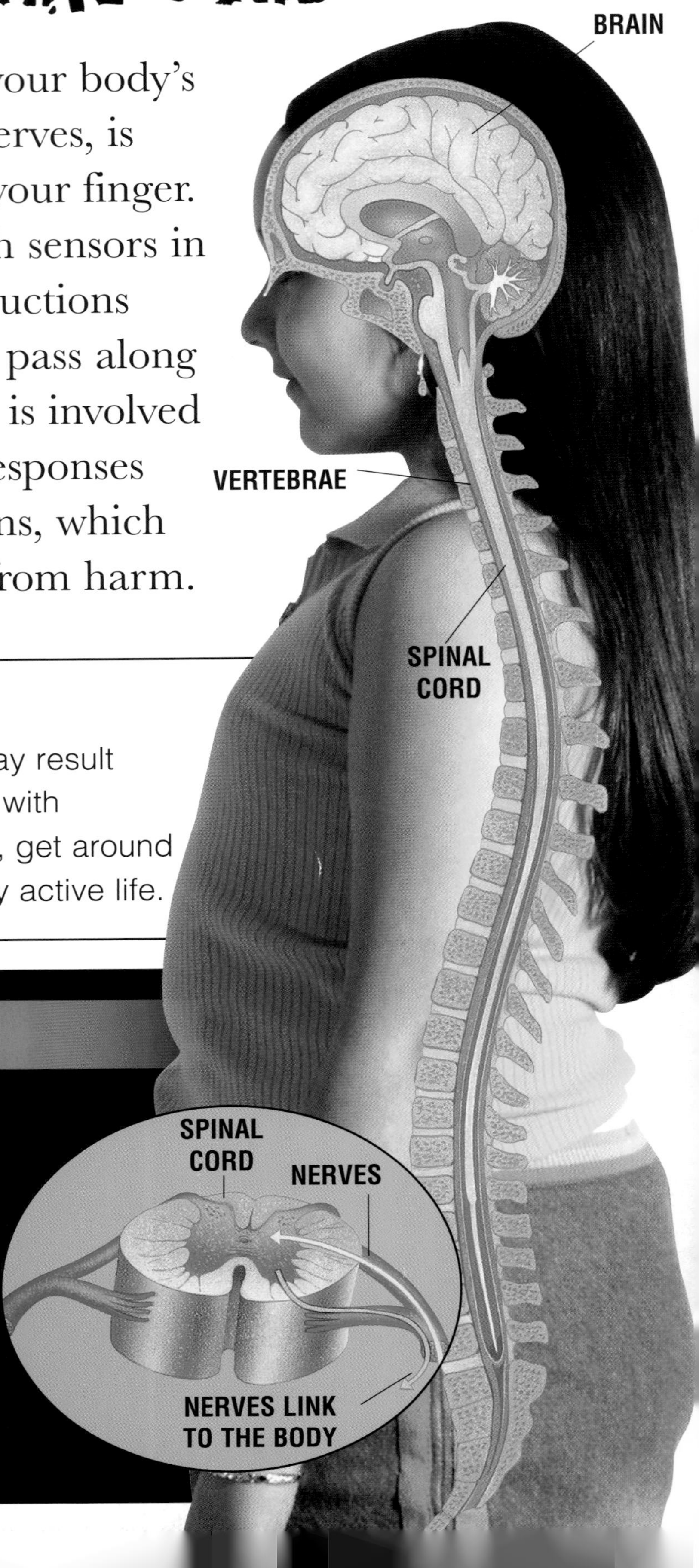

BRAIN

VERTEBRAE

SPINAL CORD

PARALYSIS

Loss of movement, paralysis, may result if the spinal cord is damaged. People with paraplegia, whose legs are paralysed, get around using wheelchairs and can lead a very active life.

PARTS OF THE SPINAL CORD

The bundle of nerves that forms your spinal cord passes through a tunnel created by holes in the separate vertebrae (bones) of your spine. The bony tunnel helps to protect the spinal cord from knocks and injury. Thirty-one pairs of nerves branch off the spinal cord to link with the rest of your body.

SPINAL CORD

NERVES

NERVES LINK TO THE BODY

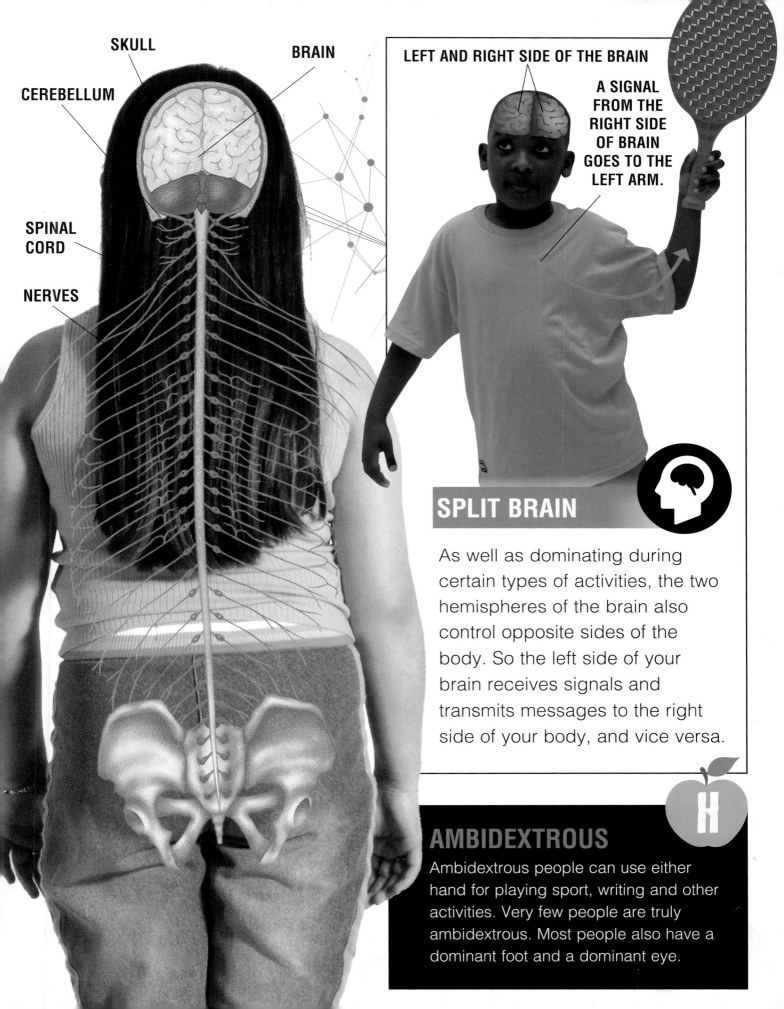

SKULL

CEREBELLUM

BRAIN

SPINAL CORD

NERVES

LEFT AND RIGHT SIDE OF THE BRAIN

A SIGNAL FROM THE RIGHT SIDE OF BRAIN GOES TO THE LEFT ARM.

SPLIT BRAIN

As well as dominating during certain types of activities, the two hemispheres of the brain also control opposite sides of the body. So the left side of your brain receives signals and transmits messages to the right side of your body, and vice versa.

AMBIDEXTROUS

Ambidextrous people can use either hand for playing sport, writing and other activities. Very few people are truly ambidextrous. Most people also have a dominant foot and a dominant eye.

WHAT ARE NERVES?

Nerves are long, thin fibres that connect your brain with the rest of your body. Like miniature electrical cables, nerves relay signals from your senses to the brain, and pass instructions from the brain to the rest of the body. Amazingly, nerve cells can transmit millions of tiny electrical pulses every second.

NERVE SIGNALS ARE VERY SPEEDY! THE FASTEST SIGNALS RACE ALONG NERVES AT SPEEDS OF UP TO 580KM PER HOUR!

NERVE STRUCTURE

Nerve cells have a central body, containing a nucleus, from which many fine dendrites (tentacles) radiate. Dendrites receive signals from other nerves. Most nerve cells also have an axon – a long tentacle that sends messages to other nerve cells.

MYELIN SHEATH

AXON

SYNAPSES

Synapses are tiny gaps between nerves, where one cell meets another. When the nerve signal reaches the end of the axon, it triggers the release of chemicals. These leap the synapse (gap) to the receptor to pass the signal on.

DENDRITE

NUCLEUS

NERVE CELL BODY

SYNAPSE

RECEPTOR

RECEPTOR

CHEMICAL MESSENGER

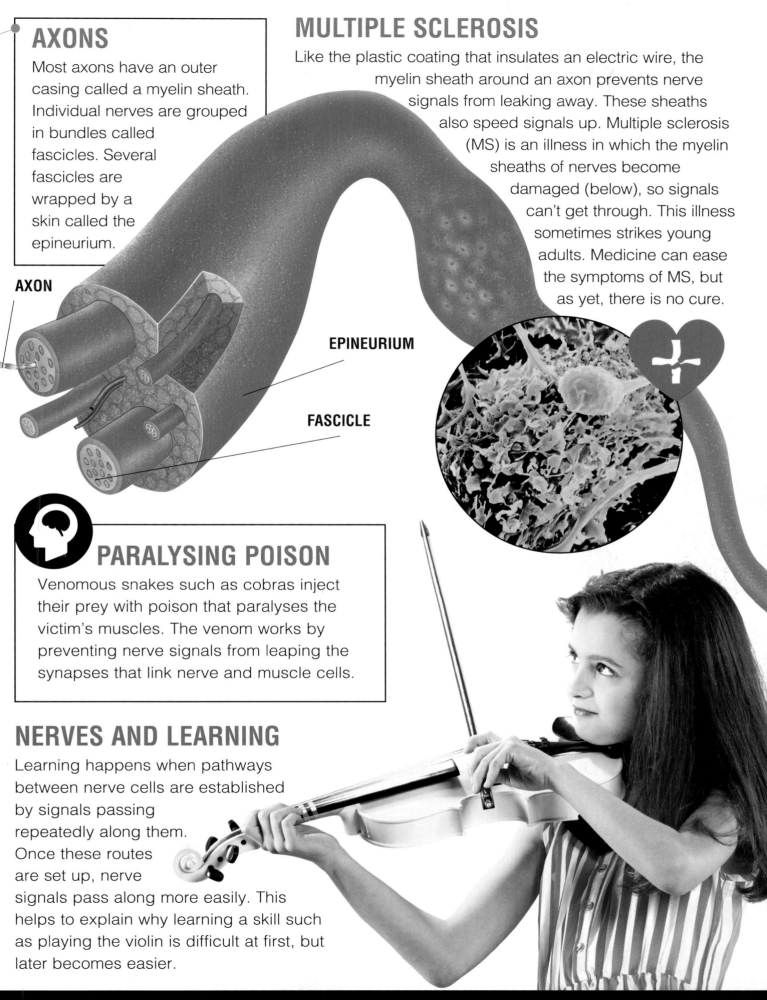

AXONS

Most axons have an outer casing called a myelin sheath. Individual nerves are grouped in bundles called fascicles. Several fascicles are wrapped by a skin called the epineurium.

AXON

EPINEURIUM

FASCICLE

MULTIPLE SCLEROSIS

Like the plastic coating that insulates an electric wire, the myelin sheath around an axon prevents nerve signals from leaking away. These sheaths also speed signals up. Multiple sclerosis (MS) is an illness in which the myelin sheaths of nerves become damaged (below), so signals can't get through. This illness sometimes strikes young adults. Medicine can ease the symptoms of MS, but as yet, there is no cure.

PARALYSING POISON

Venomous snakes such as cobras inject their prey with poison that paralyses the victim's muscles. The venom works by preventing nerve signals from leaping the synapses that link nerve and muscle cells.

NERVES AND LEARNING

Learning happens when pathways between nerve cells are established by signals passing repeatedly along them. Once these routes are set up, nerve signals pass along more easily. This helps to explain why learning a skill such as playing the violin is difficult at first, but later becomes easier.

ACTIONS AND REFLEXES

A voluntary movement is any action you choose to perform, from kicking a ball to flicking a light switch. The motor centre in your brain plans and orders your muscles to carry out these movements. Involuntary movements are movements made by the body without your conscious instructions. These include reflex actions that help protect you from danger.

NERVE STRUCTURE

When you decide to pick up a cup, information from your eyes helps your brain to locate the object precisely. The motor cortex in your brain sends signals along nerves called motor nerves to the muscles of your arm and hand. As you reach forward, your eyes and internal sensors monitor the position of your arm, to make sure the action happens smoothly. Touch sensors help your fingers to grasp the cup.

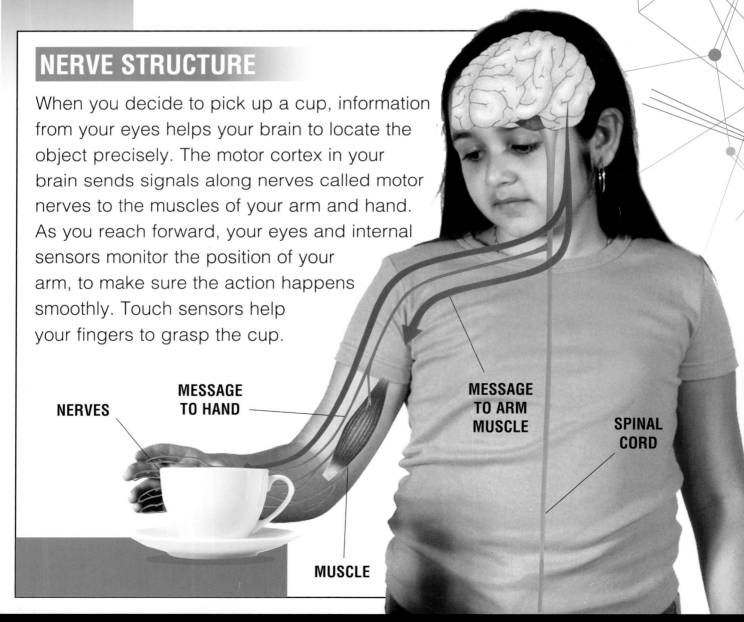

NERVES

MESSAGE TO HAND

MESSAGE TO ARM MUSCLE

SPINAL CORD

MUSCLE

TEST YOUR REFLEXES

Reflexes are lightning-fast responses that your body carries out – usually to prevent injury. They happen so quickly that there is no time for the brain to order the movement. Nerves in the spinal cord give the order instead. Test a simple reflex by getting a friend to tap your knee just below the knee cap. This tap stretches the thigh muscle. The spinal cord orders your thigh muscle to contract and your leg kicks out.

THE BLINK OF AN EYE

If you see an object speeding towards you, your body instinctively reacts to ward off the danger. You fling your arms up to protect your head from the missile. You also blink to protect your sensitive eyes.

INVOLUNTARY MOVEMENTS

If you grasp the sides of a hot cup rather than the handle, pain sensors in your fingers flash a message towards your brain. But the spinal cord reacts to the signal before it even reaches the brain. It orders your fingers to drop the cup to prevent you from getting burned. This is a reflex action. At the same time, it relays a signal to the brain to tell it what has happened.

MESSAGE TO THE BRAIN TO TELL IT WHAT HAPPENED

MESSAGE TO THE MUSCLE TO TELL IT TO DROP THE CUP

MESSAGE TO THE SPINAL CORD TO TELL IT THAT IT IS EXPERIENCING PAIN

SPINAL CORD

EVEN
WHEN
YOU ARE
ASLEEP,
YOUR
BRAIN IS
STILL
BUSY.
SOME
PEOPLE
TALK AND
EVEN
WALK IN
THEIR
SLEEP!

AUTO PILOT

Your autonomic nervous system works like the autopilot in an aircraft, regulating body processes such as breathing without you needing to think about it. Parts of the lower brain – the brain stem and the mid-brain – and also the spinal cord and many peripheral nerves are involved in this system. Your autopilot keeps your body running smoothly whether you are awake or asleep!

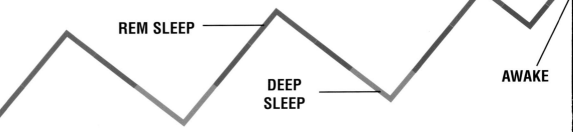

REM SLEEP

DEEP
SLEEP

AWAKE

SLEEP PATTERNS

When you sleep, your brain enters different levels of slumber. These include deep sleep and REM sleep, when the brain is more active (see page 10). At night, you pass from deep to REM sleep several times – every 60 to 90 minutes – and gradually sleep less deeply, until you wake.

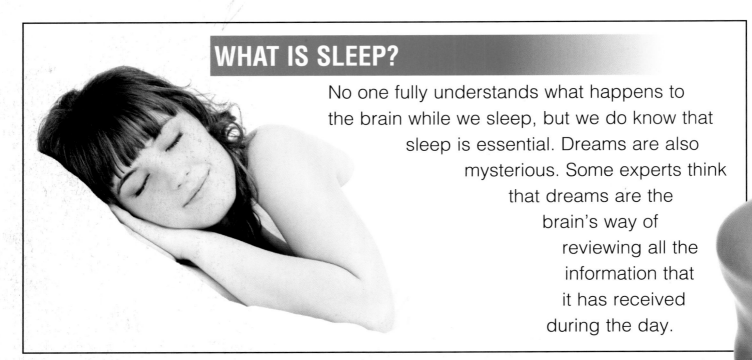

WHAT IS SLEEP?

No one fully understands what happens to the brain while we sleep, but we do know that sleep is essential. Dreams are also mysterious. Some experts think that dreams are the brain's way of reviewing all the information that it has received during the day.

AUTOMATIC NERVOUS SYSTEM

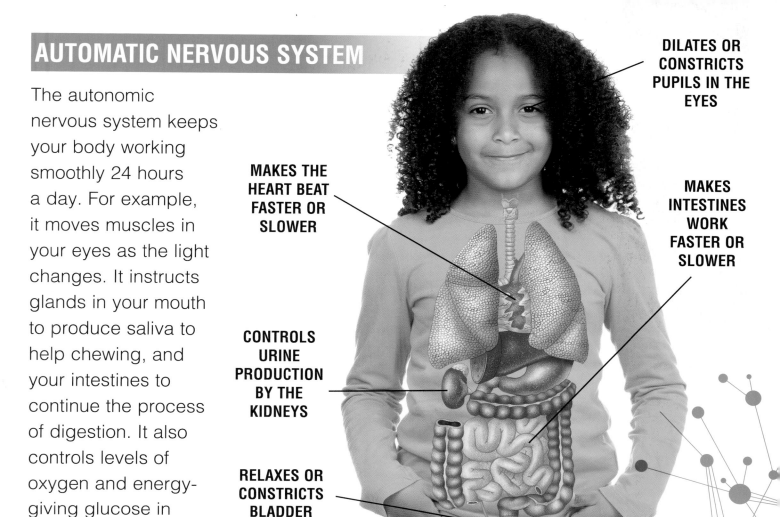

The autonomic nervous system keeps your body working smoothly 24 hours a day. For example, it moves muscles in your eyes as the light changes. It instructs glands in your mouth to produce saliva to help chewing, and your intestines to continue the process of digestion. It also controls levels of oxygen and energy-giving glucose in your blood.

DILATES OR CONSTRICTS PUPILS IN THE EYES

MAKES THE HEART BEAT FASTER OR SLOWER

MAKES INTESTINES WORK FASTER OR SLOWER

CONTROLS URINE PRODUCTION BY THE KIDNEYS

RELAXES OR CONSTRICTS BLADDER

RUNNING ON AUTOMATIC

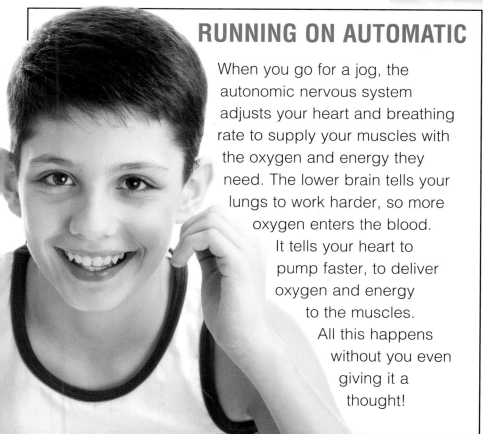

When you go for a jog, the autonomic nervous system adjusts your heart and breathing rate to supply your muscles with the oxygen and energy they need. The lower brain tells your lungs to work harder, so more oxygen enters the blood.

It tells your heart to pump faster, to deliver oxygen and energy to the muscles.

All this happens without you even giving it a thought!

UNCONSCIOUSNESS

A severe blow to the head can knock you out – make you unconscious. Afterwards, when you come round, you may feel sick and dizzy and have a headache. In extreme cases, some people even suffer from memory loss. Visit a doctor as soon as possible if you get an injury of this kind, just to check that no serious harm has been done.

YOUR SENSES – SIGHT

Sight is the main sense most people rely on to find out about their surroundings. Your eyes are jelly-filled spheres which each contain a lens that focuses light onto the back of the eye. There, a light-sensitive zone called the retina detects patterns of light, shapes and colours. This information is relayed to the brain via the optic nerve. Visual centres in the brain process the data so you can understand what you see.

INSIDE THE EYE

Over the front of the eye is a clear, dome-shaped covering called the cornea. Behind is a coloured ring called the iris, with an opening in the centre, called the pupil. Light passes through the pupil and into the eye. Muscles in the iris narrow or widen the pupil to allow more or less light into the eye.

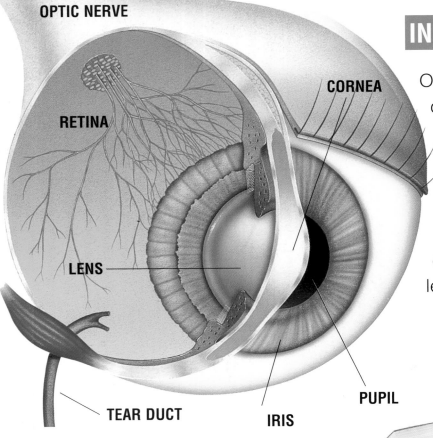

OPTIC NERVE

RETINA

CORNEA

LENS

TEAR DUCT

IRIS

PUPIL

ALTERED IMAGE

The lens focuses light onto the retina. Here, objects appear upside-down. Retinal cells convert colours and shapes into nerve signals, which are sent to the brain. The brain flips the image the right way up.

BINOCULAR VISION

Positioned several centimetres apart, your eyes each see a slightly different view. The two fields of vision overlap in a zone at the front, as shown below left. Information from each eye passes down the optic nerves to the visual centre on the opposite side of the brain. Here, the signals are decoded. Data from the overlapping area helps you to judge distances, so you can focus on a moving ball. It also gives you three-dimensional vision. If you only had one eye, everything would look much flatter.

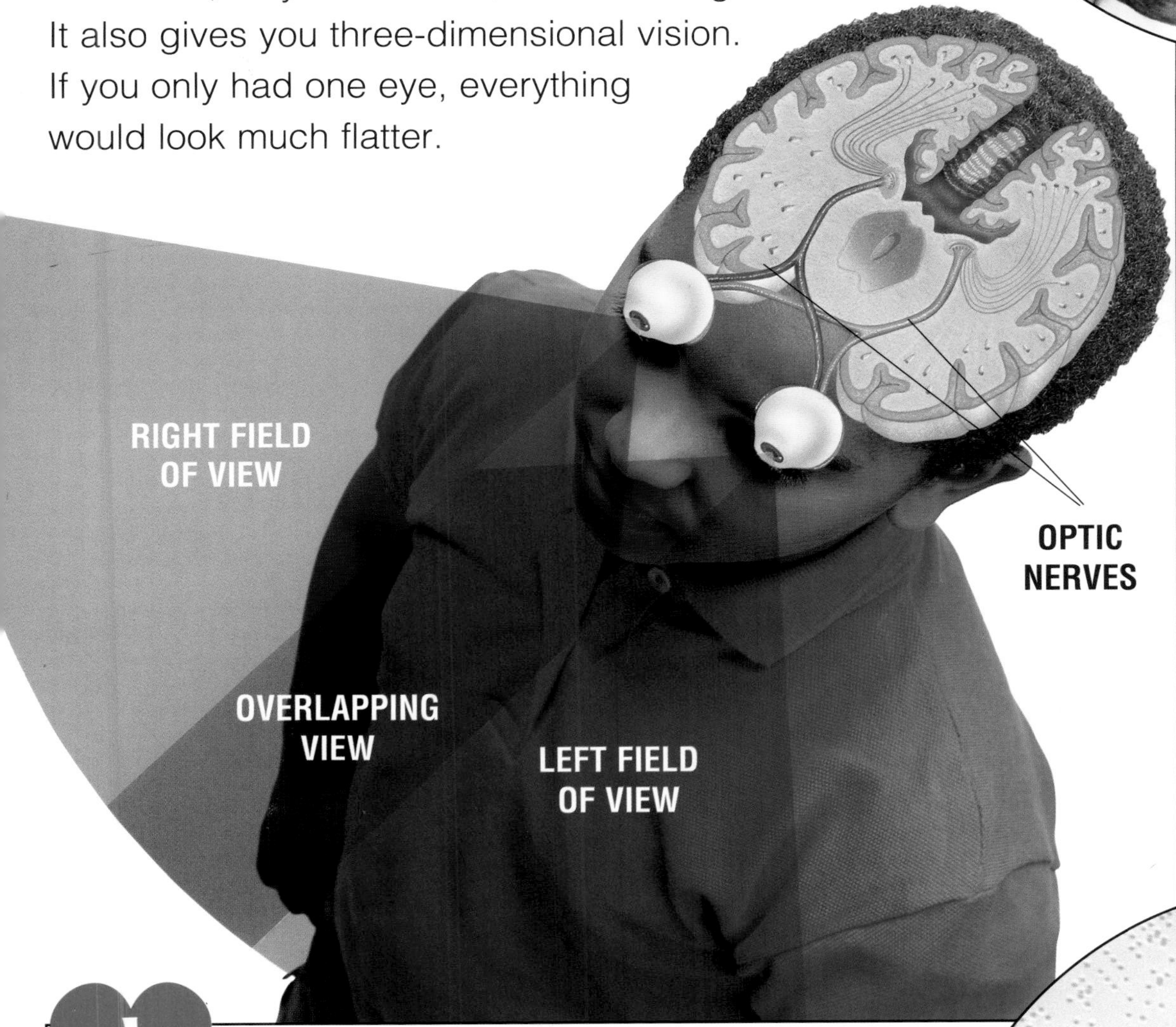

RIGHT FIELD OF VIEW

OVERLAPPING VIEW

LEFT FIELD OF VIEW

OPTIC NERVES

PROTECT YOUR EYES

Your eyes can be damaged by bright sunshine. Keep them healthy by wearing dark glasses in bright light and never look directly at the sun. Glasses and goggles also protect your eyes from dust.

BLINDNESS

Some people are blind from birth, others become blind following an accident or illness. People who are blind rely on their other senses. Touch allows them to 'read' Braille, a system of raised dots on the page.

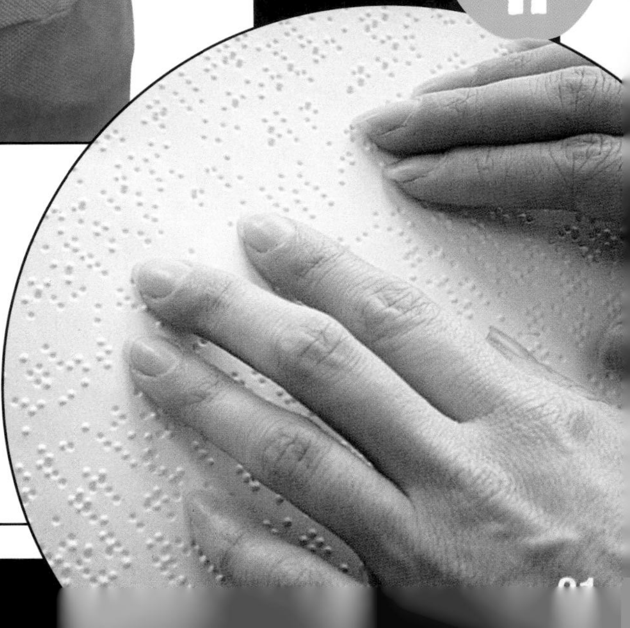

HEARING AND BALANCE

What sounds can you hear right now? Even if there are no loud noises, you can probably hear quiet sounds such as the swish of passing cars. Sound waves are vibrations passing through the air. They spread out from sound sources like ripples in a pond. When they reach your ears, you hear them. Your ears, together with your eyes and other sensors, help you to balance.

EAR PROTECTION

Your hearing can be harmed by very loud sounds such as a workman's drill or very loud music. Be careful not to turn up music too loud.

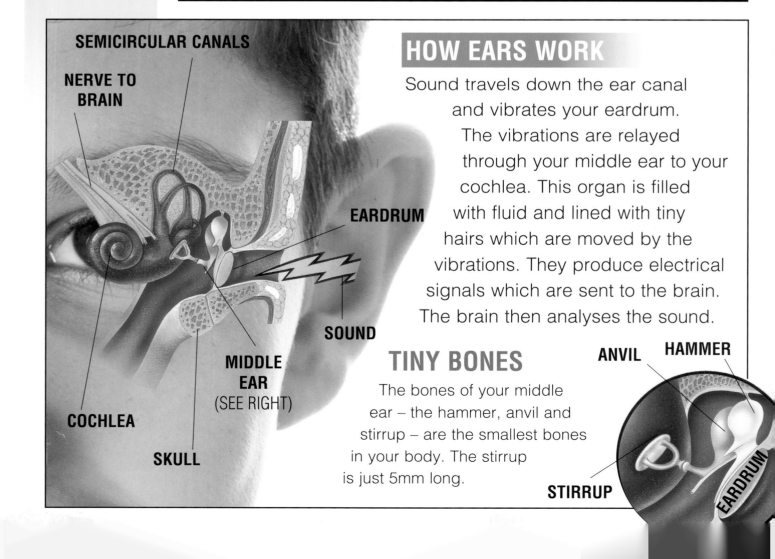

HOW EARS WORK

Sound travels down the ear canal and vibrates your eardrum. The vibrations are relayed through your middle ear to your cochlea. This organ is filled with fluid and lined with tiny hairs which are moved by the vibrations. They produce electrical signals which are sent to the brain. The brain then analyses the sound.

TINY BONES

The bones of your middle ear – the hammer, anvil and stirrup – are the smallest bones in your body. The stirrup is just 5mm long.

SEMICIRCULAR CANALS

NERVE TO BRAIN

EARDRUM

SOUND

MIDDLE EAR (SEE RIGHT)

COCHLEA

SKULL

ANVIL

HAMMER

STIRRUP

EARDRUM

BALANCE SENSORS

Information from your eyes, skin, ears and other sensors help you to balance. The balance organs of the ears are three fluid-filled loops called semicircular canals. These are positioned at right-angles to one another so the fluid in at least one canal swirls whichever way you tilt your head. Nerves from the semicircular canals send messages to the brain to let it know which way up your head is.

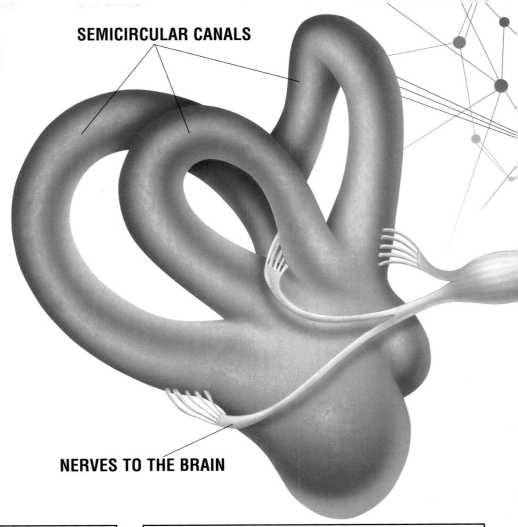

SEMICIRCULAR CANALS

NERVES TO THE BRAIN

DEAFNESS

Some people are born deaf, others become deaf later in life because of illness or injury. A hearing aid, which amplifies sounds, can help some people with hearing difficulties. Many deaf people also use sign language and lip reading to communicate with others. Anyone can learn sign language – why not give it a try?

PITCH

The pitch of a sound is how high or low it is. High and low sounds produce sound waves of different frequencies. A high sound vibrates faster than a low sound – its frequency is higher. Pitch is measured in hertz (Hz). Human beings can hear sounds between 20 and 20,000 Hz. Animals such as dogs, bats and dolphins can hear sounds with pitches higher than this.

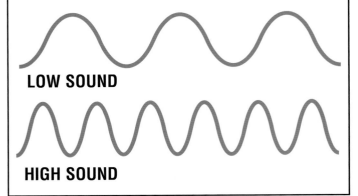

LOW SOUND

HIGH SOUND

TASTE, SMELL AND TOUCH

Your senses of taste and smell allow you to savour food – think how boring meals would be if you couldn't taste! Both senses may also detect danger signs, from the tell-tale whiff of smoke to the taste of bad food. Touch is another vital sense. A collection of several different touch sensations convey all sorts of information about the outside world.

BITTER

SOUR

SALTY

SWEET

TASTING

Taste buds are tiny bumps on your tongue. You have around 10,000 of these little bumps, which detect four main flavours: sweet, sour, salt and bitter. Your saliva dissolves the flavours in food so you can taste it. The four flavours are sensed in different parts of your tongue, as shown. Taste buds are also found on the roof of your mouth, in your cheeks and upper throat. If you lose your sense of smell, your sense of taste is affected too.

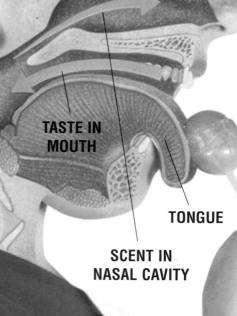

TASTE IN MOUTH

TONGUE

SCENT IN NASAL CAVITY

FEELING PAIN

Pain is what you feel when your body is being damaged. Painkillers are very useful! Modern medicine has developed all sorts of painkillers. Dentists inject you with an anaesthetic before working on your teeth.

SMELLING

Smells are odour particles floating in the air. Your nose can distinguish up to 10,000 different odours! As you breathe in, scent molecules in the air waft through your nostrils to enter your nasal cavity. On the roof of the cavity are two small sensitive patches, the olfactory bulbs, lined with tiny hairs. These detect scents, like the stink of rotting fruit, and send signals to your brain, which interprets them as smells.

SCENT-SENSING ORGANS

The thumbnail-sized olfactory bulbs have tiny hairs called cilia. The hairs stick out into the mucus that lines the nasal cavity. Scent particles caught on the hairs are detected by millions of microscopic smelling cells.

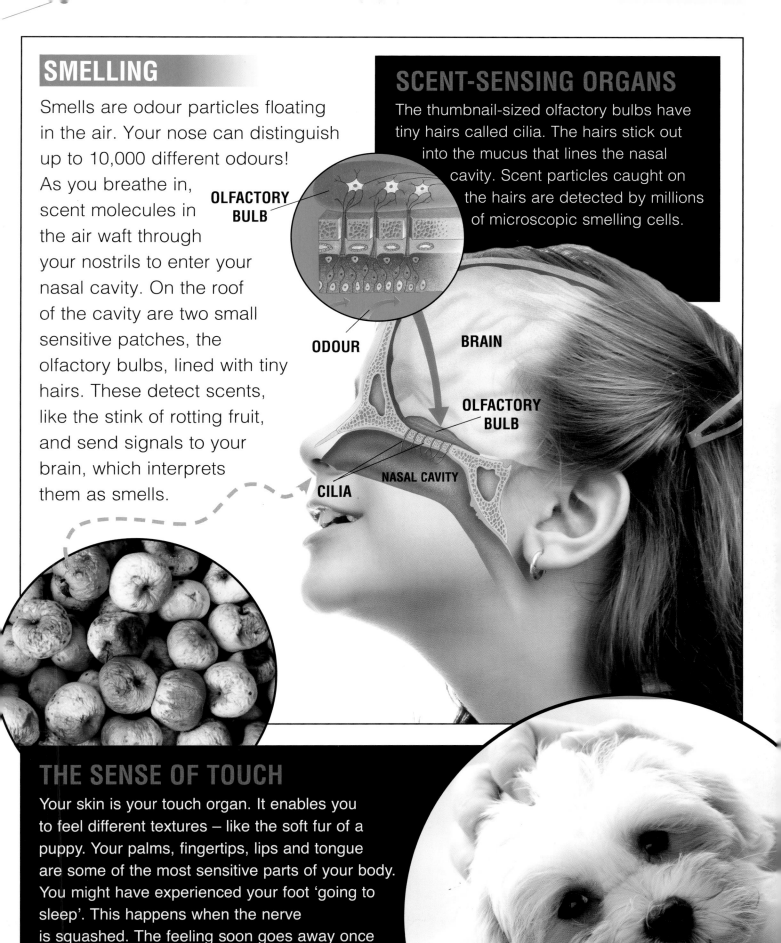

OLFACTORY BULB

ODOUR

BRAIN

OLFACTORY BULB

NASAL CAVITY

CILIA

THE SENSE OF TOUCH

Your skin is your touch organ. It enables you to feel different textures – like the soft fur of a puppy. Your palms, fingertips, lips and tongue are some of the most sensitive parts of your body. You might have experienced your foot 'going to sleep'. This happens when the nerve is squashed. The feeling soon goes away once the pressure is removed from the nerve.

BRAIN AND SENSES THROUGH LIFE

You were born with all the brain cells you will ever need – about 100 billion of them! As more connections between brain cells are established, so you learn about the world. A baby's senses are very keen, but its brain has to learn how to make sense of all the information. As you grow older, your senses gradually become less keen.

BABY DEVELOPMENT

Babies are born with various instinctive reflexes which aid survival. One is a sucking reflex, so it can gain nourishment from milk. Gradually, the child learns to make sense of sights, sounds, smells, tastes and other sensations. It learns to focus and recognise faces, and later starts to babble and finally talk.

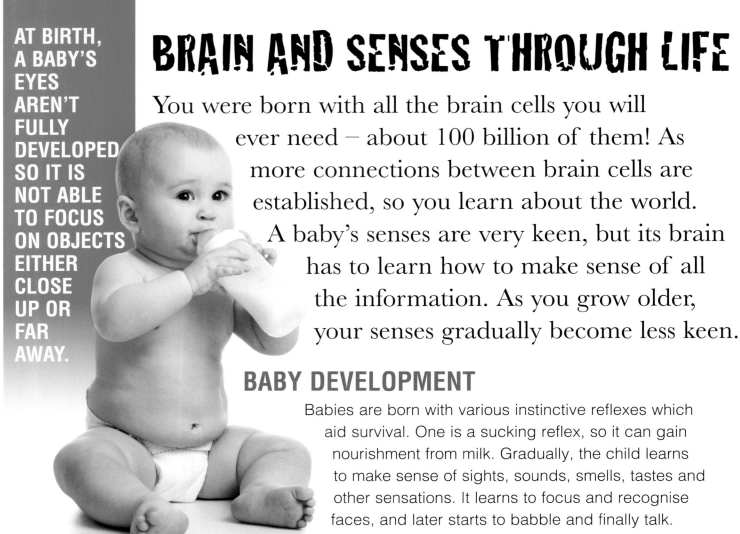

THE GROWING BRAIN

The brain of an unborn baby starts to develop early. At just three weeks into its development, a lump of nerve tissue in the head begins to develop into the cerebrum, cerebellum and other brain parts. Meanwhile the spinal cord and the rest of the nervous system also develop. By the time the baby is ready to be born all parts of the brain are formed, even the wrinkles in the cerebral cortex.

3 WEEKS

6 WEEKS

3 MONTHS

9 MONTHS (BIRTH)

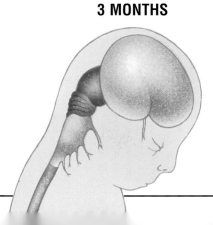

LEARNING

Learning happens as connections are made between brain cells. Each nerve cell can form up to 10,000 of these links with other cells, so the total number of connections that can be made is huge. Children can absorb a lot of information daily, so learning is relatively easy. Around the age of 20, your brain cells start to die off, so it gets harder to learn. However, you have plenty of cells to spare!

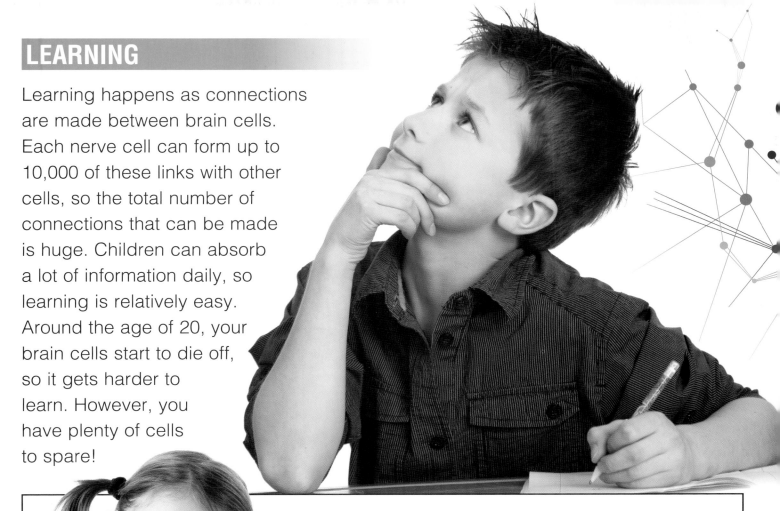

WEARING GLASSES

People of any age can be short- or long-sighted. This is when the eyeball is either elongated or squashed. As a result, the image isn't focussed directly on the retina. Glasses or contact lenses change the focus so that the image falls squarely on the retina, so you can see clearly. Visit the optician regularly to keep your eyes in tiptop condition.

ALZHEIMER'S DISEASE

Alzheimer's disease is an illness which affects the brain. It is most common in older people. Connections between nerve cells are disturbed, causing memory loss, mood swings and loss of muscle control. Old photos are sometimes used to help the patient remember details about their life. Doctors have not yet found a cure for Alzheimer's.

STAYING HEALTHY

Your brain and senses are truly amazing. Keep your brain, senses, and the rest of your body in top condition by eating a healthy diet, taking regular exercise and avoiding illegal drugs. Using your brain keeps it active, so use it as much as you can. Like other parts of your body, your brain and senses can sometimes go wrong. The brain can be affected by illness or by emotional problems, but medicine or counselling can often help.

THE EFFECT OF DRUGS

Illegal drugs affect your brain and senses. Even legal drugs such as alcohol and tobacco interfere with natural body functions and change the balance of chemicals in your brain. Some drugs are addictive and can damage your health.

DEALING WITH DEPRESSION

Everyone has worries and feels low from time to time. But some young people have a more serious problem with depression. Periods when they feel sad and hopeless may alternate with times when they are manic – ultra-energetic. Depression may be caused by an imbalance in brain chemistry, or by emotional problems. Seeing a professional counsellor or psychiatrist, or taking medicine prescribed by a doctor, can help.

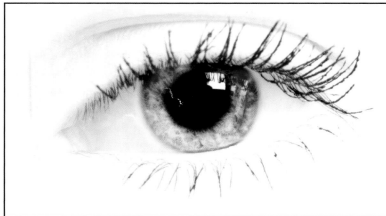

EYE TEST

Parts of your body, such as your eyes and teeth, benefit from regular check-ups to stay healthy. A visit to the optician will sort out any eye problems and can also pick up other illnesses. See a doctor if you experience any problems with other senses such as hearing or balance.

BLOOD VESSELS

STRESS

We all feel stressed every now and then. Talking over your troubles with a friend, parent or another trusted adult can help. If you are being bullied, tell an adult. Yoga, a programme of calming exercises, and meditation, a technique for focusing the mind, can help to ease stress. Other people prefer playing an energetic sport!

MIGRAINES

Migraines are very bad headaches which can be brought on by stress, drugs such as alcohol, or even foods like chocolate. As the blood vessels to the brain narrow, the brain's blood supply is reduced. As well as a thumping headache, the sufferer may feel sick and have distorted vision. Migraines are quite a common problem. See your doctor if you have symptoms like these.

The spinal cord, the body's main nerve, measures about 45 cm long in adults.

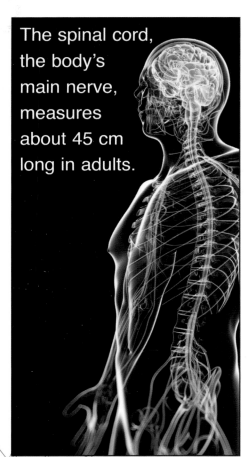

Bats have poor sight, but use super-sensitive hearing to catch insects. Rattlesnakes can sense the body heat of animals, which they use to catch prey. Birds and whales can sense the Earth's magnetic field, which they use to find their way.

After the age of 20, over 10,000 of your brain cells die off every day, which makes learning a bit more difficult. So learn lots while you can!

AMAZING FACTS

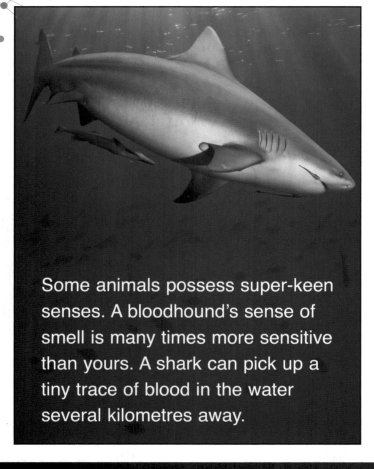

Some animals possess super-keen senses. A bloodhound's sense of smell is many times more sensitive than yours. A shark can pick up a tiny trace of blood in the water several kilometres away.

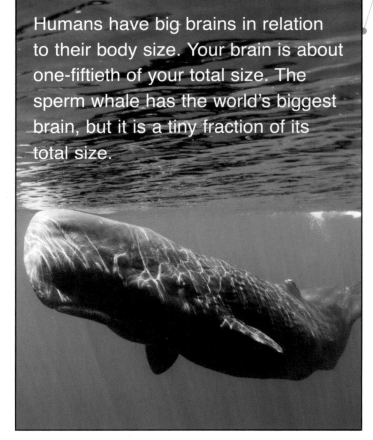

Humans have big brains in relation to their body size. Your brain is about one-fiftieth of your total size. The sperm whale has the world's biggest brain, but it is a tiny fraction of its total size.

GLOSSARY

AUTONOMIC NERVOUS SYSTEM Part of the nervous system that controls automatic functions such as breathing and digestion.

AXON A long, thin extension to a nerve cell which relays instructions from the brain.

CENTRAL NERVOUS SYSTEM Part of the nervous system, made up of the brain and spinal cord.

CEREBELLUM Part of the brain below the cerebrum, which helps with balance and coordination.

CEREBRUM The upper brain, which is divided into two halves called cerebral hemispheres.

COCHLEA A coiling, fluid-filled tube in your inner ear which changes sounds into nerve signals and so helps you to hear.

CEREBRAL CORTEX The wrinkled outer layer of the cerebrum where thought takes place.

DENDRITE A long, thin tentacle extending from a nerve cell, which receives signals from other nerves.

MOTOR CORTEX A part of the cerebral cortex which orders voluntary (conscious) movements.

NERVE One of the long, thin fibres that carry signals to and from the brain.

NEURON A nerve cell, which receives and transmits nerve impulses.

OLFACTORY ORGAN A small, sensitive patch on the roof of the cavity inside your nose that detects smells.

PERIPHERAL NERVOUS SYSTEM The vast network of tiny nerves that reach every part of the body.

REFLEX ACTION A rapid, automatic movement that usually helps to protect the body from injury.

RETINA A light-sensitive zone in the back of the eye, which relays information about shapes and colours to the brain.

SEMICIRCULAR CANAL One of three fluid-filled loops in your inner ear, which help you to balance.

SPINAL CORD The body's main bundle of nerves, which runs down inside the backbone to link the brain with smaller nerves throughout the body.

TASTE BUD One of the tiny sensors on your tongue, cheeks or throat that detects flavours in food, and so allows you to taste.

SYNAPSE A tiny gap between two nerve cells.

INDEX

Photocredits

Abbreviations: l–left, r-right, b–bottom, t-top, c-centre, m–middle, ba–background

All photos supplied by PBD Except for:
Front cover – CLIPAREA l Custom media / Shutterstock.com. 3bl – Rainer Plendl /Shutterstock.com. 4tr – both Digital Stock. 7l – gosphotodesign / Shutterstock.com. 8bl, 31br – VaLiza /Shutterstock.com. 9tr – Gladskikh Tatiana./Shutterstock.com. 9c – Zephyr/Science Photo Library. 10ml – Maks Narodenko /Shutterstock.com. 10mr –Plus69/Shutterstock.com. 11mr – GJLP. 13tr – Roger Vlitos. 15tr – Dr John Zajicek/Science Photo Library. 15br – Helder Almeida/Shutterstock.com. 16bl – Sergey Peterman/Shutterstock.com. 17br – ifong/Shutterstock.com. 18bl – artfamily/Shutterstock.com. 19tr – Gelpi JM/Shutterstock.com. 19bl, 22bl – SergiyN/Shutterstock.com. 20br– RogerVlitos. 21tr – Alinute Silzeviciute/Shutterstock.com. 21c– RogerVlitos. 21br – Larry Mulvehil. 23bl – Alan Poulson Photography/Shutterstock.com. 24ml – Dmitry Naumov/Shutterstock.com. 24mr – Kamira/Shutterstock.com. 25br – Calvin Chan /Shutterstock.com. 26tl – Oksana Kuzmina/Shutterstock.com. 27tr – Rainer Plendl/Shutterstock.com. 27ml – iko/Shutterstock.com. 27br – PathDoc/Shutterstock.com. 28mr – nikkytok/Shutterstock.com. 28bl – Corel. 29tr – mashe/Shutterstock.com. 29c – Mikael Damkier/Shutterstock.com. 30bl — Willyam Bradberry/Shutterstock.com. 30br — Shane Gross/Shutterstock.com. 30tl — Sebastian Kaulitzki/Shutterstock.com. 30tc — Nashepard/Shutterstock.com. 30tr — Ollyy/Shutterstock.com